NATIONAL GEOGRAPHIC

T0061010

# Signs on the Way

Marvin Buckley

Dad and I are going to the hospital.

We see this sign on the way.

This sign tells us how fast we can drive.

We see this sign on the way.

This sign tells us to stop for other cars.

We see this sign on the way.

This sign tells us to slow down for roadwork.

We see this sign on the way.

This sign tells us what street we are on.

We see this sign on the way.

This sign tells us we are near the hospital.

We see this sign on the way.

This sign tells us where
to find my new baby brother.